Discover the Rain Forest

by Lisa Trumbauer

Consultant: Steve Dodd, Director,
Park Ranger Training Program, Northern Arizona University

Yellow
Umbrella
Books
for early readers

Yellow Umbrella Books are published by Red Brick Learning
7825 Telegraph Road, Bloomington, Minnesota 55438
http://www.redbricklearning.com

Editorial Director: Mary Lindeen
Senior Editor: Hollie J. Endres
Photo Researcher: Signature Design
Developer: Raindrop Publishing
Consultant: Steve Dodd, Director, Park Ranger Training Program, Northern Arizona University
Conversion Assistants: Jenny Marks, Laura Manthe

J 578.734
Trumbauer

Library of Congress Cataloging-in-Publication Data
Trumbauer, Lisa, 1963-
  Discover the Rain Forest / by Lisa Trumbauer
      p. cm.
  ISBN 0-7368-5828-8 (hardcover)
  ISBN 0-7368-5258-1 (softcover)
  1. Rain forest ecology—Juvenile literature. 2. Rain forests—Juvenile literature. I. Title.
II. Series.
  QH541.5.R27T79 2005
  578.734—dc22

                                        2005016137

Photo Credits:
Cover: Comstock Photos; Title Page: Chase Swift/Corbis; Page 2: Wolfgang Kaehler/Corbis;
Page 3: Brand X Pictures; Page 4: Corel; Page 5: Corbis; Page 6: Natphotos/Digital Vision
Photos; Page 7: (left) Marion Brenner/Botanica (right) Paul Harris/Stone; Page 8: Corel; Page 9:
(left and right) Jupiter Images; Page 10: Inga Spence/Index Stock Imagery; Page 11: Theo
Allofs/Corbis; Page 12: D. Holdsworth/Robert Harding World Imagery; Page 13: Owen
Franken/Corbis; Page 14: Miguel Alvarez/Reuters Photo Archive; Page 15: John
Banagan/Lonely Planet Images

1 2 3 4 5 6 11 10 09 08 07 06

Table of Contents

What Is a Rain Forest?

A **rain forest** is an area that gets a lot of rain all year long. Most rain forests are tropical. They are found along the **equator**.

The biggest tropical rain forest in the world is in South America. The **Amazon River** runs through it. Let's discover the Amazon rain forest!

Plants of the Rain Forest

A tropical rain forest is full of plants.
The wet, warm weather is the perfect
climate for plants to grow and thrive.

The rain forest floor is dark and shadowy. Not much sunlight gets through. Plants that live here do not need much sunlight to survive.

Some rain forest trees do not grow very tall. Other trees are giants! They tower at more than 100 feet (30.5 meters). These tall trees poke through the top of the forest.

Many types of **orchids** grow on the branches of the trees. Vines called **lianas** also grow up the tree trunks. They climb upward toward the sun.

orchids

lianas

Animals of the Rain Forest

Animals live in different parts of the rain forest. **Capybaras** live along the rain forest floor. Ants, frogs, and jaguars live here, too.

In the middle layer of the rain forest, you might see scarlet macaws. An emerald tree boa wraps around a branch. It blends in with the leaves.

scarlet macaw   emerald tree boa

Many rain forest animals are expert tree climbers. Sloths move slowly along tree branches. They spend most of their time in the trees, eating leaves.

Howler monkeys grip tree branches with their hands, feet, and tails. They make loud, howling noises in the treetops.

People of the Rain Forest

For thousands of years, people have also lived in the Amazon rain forest. They used the trees of the rain forest to build their homes.

Explorers from Europe arrived in the rain forest about 500 years ago. Life in the rain forest began to change after the explorers arrived.

Many people worry about the survival
of the rain forest because so many trees
are being cut down. The trees are used
for building and making things such as
furniture.

The rain forest is an amazing, diverse **ecosystem**. With so many plants and animals, the rain forest still has many mysteries to be discovered.

Glossary

Amazon River—river in South America; one of the largest in the world.

climate—the weather of a particular area

ecosystem—all the plants and animals that make up an area

equator—an imaginary line that goes around the middle of Earth

liana—a type of vine

orchid—a type of flower

rain forest—a thick forest where it rains all year long

Index

Word Count: 351
Early-Intervention Level: K